So Many Miracles

One Woman's Conversion to Mormonism – Her Humor, Her Journey, Her Gratitude

D. Ann Nadeau

With special gratitude to
Matt Ottosen of azaerophoto.com
for use of the cover photograph.

In loving memory of

Dennis P. Blackhurst

Acknowledgement

For my students at Mountain View High

1978-1985

INTRODUCTION
Conversion: A Tricky Business

The word conversion has at least seventeen separate meanings. I know this because I just looked it up on my app. *Dictionary.com* so it must be true. After all, *Dictionary.com* has that cute little blue icon with the uppercase D in the middle and those rays jutting from it that I can only assume are a visual reference to enlightenment through knowledge. Plus it's right there on my Samsung.

The meaning that seems to define my story best is #5:

'... a change of attitude, emotion, or viewpoint from one of indifference, disbelief, or antagonism to one of acceptance, faith, or enthusiastic support, especially such a change in a person's religion...'

My indifference, disbelief and antagonism might also be labeled arrogance and fear. Whether the arrogance was an unconscious effort to hide my fear, or the fear stemmed from a lack of knowledge – knowledge being only as good as information received – I cannot say for certain.

For example, if I go to a mechanic who misdiagnoses the problem with my car, is it his fault if he truly believed his diagnosis? What if the mechanic has been inadequately trained by a person in whom he has faith? His information is inaccurate, but his intent was not to deceive. The same mechanic might eventually discover the shortcomings of his training and seek further instruction from a more reliable source.

It is only at that point that the mechanic can make the decision to continue as before or move forward. Having not realized there was a forward to move to prior to the new knowledge.

This is where it gets tricky. This is where fear resides. On the one hand, if the mechanic admits his mistakes he could risk a lawsuit. On the other hand, he could continue with his old ways, probably still make a decent living and save face. What to do? What to do?

I'm not a mechanic, and I understand that eventually most analogies, if taken to their logical extension, break down (much like that car).

The blessing of *my* new knowledge came disguised, not in the form of a problematic engine, but that of a life unraveling. Mine to be precise. I had a choice: to either continue on my self-destructive path or find another way. I'd like to tell you that I sought Father's will, but I did not. It was the pain of constant turmoil that brought me to my knees; I just wanted God to make it all go away. Looking back on it now, I see that it was my turn to hear the gospel; the Lord put His arm on my back, and gently guided me to His church knowing I was ready to hear the truth.

Whether or not I embraced it after that, was up to me. Like the mechanic, I needed to decide – stay where I was, or find a better way chancing more than a lawsuit. Chancing everything. Not only all of that which I believed before, but also those who supported me in my old beliefs.

This is my story to date. All the events are true. Only one name has been changed at the request of the person.

CHAPTER 1: Teeth and Tunes

Although I was born in Yonkers, I grew up in the Boston area, and the only thing I knew about Mormons was they sang on the radio around Christmastime. Then Donny and Marie Osmond got their own television show, and someone said they were Mormon. So I figured they had broken away from the singing group to get their own show. Now, I knew *two* things about Mormons – they sang, and they had a great deal of teeth. (Many years later, I met Marie Osmond who, gracious and funny, reminded me I had the same amount of teeth.)

My family was...my family. My mother, married six times (hey, everyone needs a hobby) did the best she could, and I'm grateful for her; she taught me a lot, including faith and prayer. But let me put it this way: if we had Family Home Evening, while I was growing up, the first thing we would do is hide all the pointy objects.

I met my future husband in high school. We dated for eight years. To say I was a little gun-shy about marriage is an understatement. Anyway, we finally married.

We drank. We fought. We drank some more.

Then, in 1978, we decided what we really needed to do to be happy, was move to a warmer climate. In some circles, this is known as *geographical therapy.* It doesn't work. You can pack up your clothes, your furniture and all your stuff, looking forward to a future free of the troubles you have convinced yourself will vanish the moment you are in a dry climate and new home. But somehow the problems manage to worm their way into the crates, and once at their new location, surprise you at how readily they acclimate themselves. Probably didn't help that we also packed up our bar. But let's move on.

We ended up in Mesa, Arizona – a burgeoning town southeast of Phoenix with Monopoly buildings and a sandy, beige game board beckoning thousands of frozen Easterners just like ourselves to come play. We loved it. What's not to love? Tennis in 115 degree heat, and second degree burns from opening your car door. I got a job teaching theatre, drama, public speaking, and debate at a new high school a mile from our Monopoly house with pool (take that Park Place!)

It was at this new high school that I began to notice some interesting differences with quite a few of my students. Differences that I hadn't seen in other schools where I had worked. Don't get me wrong, I loved teaching and I loved the students I taught back East. They were good kids, with great families that worked hard to give their children an exceptional education.

But this new breed I kept encountering in the desert? I don't know; somehow they seemed, happier, more centered.

Sunstroke? Maybe. Whatever it was, it was fascinating, and I began to ask questions.

CHAPTER 2: The Fluffies

Turns out the kids I asked about were LDS. Now, I knew what LSD was – having had some up close and personal experiences with it - but this was different. This was Latter-Day Saints - or Mormons. It was a religion.

A religion? Hmmm.

'A cult", I was told. *'But, don't worry'*, people said. *'If you aren't one of them, they ignore you.'*

This was fascinating. More questions arose as I observed these 'cultists' during class, especially when they didn't know I was watching. Were culty people always that happy and confident? Did they talk about their families in a positive way, or support other students who performed for class?

I didn't have any answers, but after a while I developed a kind of Mormon radar, and when the non-LDS kids challenged me to try and pick out Mormons in the yearbook, (sort of like *Where's Waldo* only with bigger smiles, and fewer striped beanies*)* my accuracy rate was pretty impressive.

At about this time, Dean and Geraldine, our best friends, as well as serious drinking buddies, moved from Florida to Mesa. We took turns spending Sundays at each other's houses where we played cards and drank. Trust me, we were better at the drinking than the cards. We were so good at it that that whole rest on the Sabbath thing? We took that *quite* seriously. So seriously in fact, that at least one of us would pass out. That's how rested we were. But prior to passing out, while we played cards, we'd watch a weekly phenomenon take place outside our front windows.

People would parade by. Fluffy people in fluffy dresses, with fluffy hair, and fluffy ties looking a lot like little families of ducks with books tucked under their wings. So we called them, what else? The Fluffies. And there were lots of them. In Mesa, Arizona, Mormon chapels are a lot like Starbucks – there's one on every corner.

Part of my job as a Theatre Arts teacher, was to train and supervise a paid crew to design and install lights as well as sound whenever any organization in the community rented the theatre. One such group was from what its members referred to as a *stake building*. Of course, I assumed it was a restaurant with a rather unimaginative name, but no; a stake is a number of wards (like parishes) included in a region. One local LDS 'stake' wanted to produce a play called *Aurelia,* celebrating the 100-year anniversary of the founding of the LDS children's organization by Aurelia Spencer Rogers.

The day the co-directors came to my office to discuss the project, I found myself sitting across from the two fluffiest women I had ever seen.

CHAPTER 3: First Class Mission

As rehearsals began, I was instantly taken by, not just the two Fluffies' (Rose Mary and Becky) work ethic, but by that of all the Fluffies that showed up to help. Parents came after work, children (Fluffettes) after school. Everyone, from the youngest to the oldest, had an assignment. There were no divas, no excuses, no whiners; and I have to tell you, in the theatre, even at a high school level, that is rare. The kids brought their homework, and in between stage time, helped each other with assignments, cleaned up when rehearsal was over, replaced something if it was broken, and hit every deadline.

With all of that, the one thing with which I was most impressed was the way Fluffies spoke to each other. They were respectful and kind, taking immediate responsibility for whatever went wrong and fixing it. Okay, so they used the words *Brother* and *Sister* a lot, which might lead one to believe Mormons are an Amish off-shoot. Still, I was impressed.

One thing I did not understand - at all - was why these two Fluffy women, Rose Mary and Becky, even after the production was over, insisted on being my friend. Aside from a love of theatre, we didn't seem to have anything else in common. Still they invited my husband and I on triple dates with them and their husbands, or to play tennis; and Rose Mary, even invited me to join a women's organization.

Looking back on it now, I realize I wasn't comfortable around Fluffies. I kept thinking I was going to say something inappropriate which I'm sure I did, but I never once got the feeling I was being judged.

Maybe the real problem was *me*.

The following year I decided to take my advanced acting class to New York for spring break to see Broadway shows. We sold hot chocolate, cookies, and snow cones. We held a raffle, sponsored a midnight horror movie, washed cars, begged, and cajoled. Finally, we had enough money. I filled out the necessary forms, and a few days later got a letter from the superintendent's office which read: *'We are not running a travel agency'.*

Normally, something like that would have stopped me, or at least it would stop anyone who valued her job, or tenure, which I had yet to earn, but for some reason, I became more determined.

My husband Jerry said, "Let it go. It's not worth it."

I couldn't. So, I took it to the school board, where members over-rode the superintendent – what was I thinking? The members thought it was a great opportunity for the students and OK'd it right away, with one stipulation, that

I get another adult, besides myself, to chaperone the eleven students. One, of the eleven, was Rose Mary's oldest daughter.

Yep, I asked the fluffy lady.

The day came, and all thirteen of us (eleven hyper students and two strangely matched adults) were sitting in our seats ready to take off when the pilot came over the intercom to announce, 'I'm sorry, but we have overbooked this flight. If anyone would like to get off this flight, and get on the next one, we will give each of you $150.00.'

Well, two of my students almost killed themselves running down the aisle to disembark. Of course I stopped them. Hey, I might have been a drunk, but I knew enough not to have two kids on one coast and nine on the other.

"Look, if there is enough for all of us okay," I said. "If not, we can't do it."

There were fourteen seats needed. We all got off, plus one other passenger, each received $150.00, waited two hours, and got on the next flight. By now, the kids were uncontrollable thinking about all they would do with that extra cash. In 1980, $150.00 was a *lot* of money, especially to teenagers. Today? One t-shirt and a street pretzel – tops.

After Rose Mary and I were buckled in for a second time, a flight attendant approached us. "Are you the chaperones for this group?" I have to tell you, I almost lied not knowing what one of the kids might have already done with the money. "We're so sorry for the inconvenience. Would you like to sit in First Class?"

What are you kidding me?

"Well, that would be nice," I said, and picking up my plastic tote bag with *Smith's Food Stores* in bright red across the front, Rose Mary and I moved to First Class.

You know what is so neat about First Class? I mean, aside from the fact that your entire backside fits in the seat, and the silverware doesn't snap when you use it? For the next seven hours, I wasn't going to hear: 'Mrs. Nadeau! Mrs. Nadeau! Mrs. Nadeau!' Not one of my students could bug me, because when the flight attendant pulls that curtain across the great divide, the peons are not allowed to co-mingle with the…uhm….what are we called up there? The Non-Peons. Yes, that's it. The Non-Peons! (Notice how I capitalized?) What do you talk about on a coast-to-coast flight when you are sitting next to the world's biggest Fluffy?

"So, how did you get so fluffy?" I asked.

CHAPTER 4: It's Up For Debate

I wanted to know all there was about these Mormons, and Rose Mary began by telling me about a young boy who wanted to know truth. How he knelt down, in the clearing of a grove to pray, and how God answered his prayers.

Having taught junior high, I saw first-hand the struggle young teenagers go through questioning everything around them. They just want to know. I myself began questioning my own faith at that age, leading me to a twenty-year search including a philosophy minor in college. Then again, it was the 60's – everyone was a philosopher. And the one thing I knew, after all that time? If there was such a thing as truth, everything else would fall into place.

During that flight, as my new friend shared her testimony, I began to feel the tumblers move.

Rose Mary has said I asked 'all the right questions.' I must have, because by the time we reached New York, I knew something was happening.

That week we saw five plays, ate at Sardis, went to museums, bemoaned the subway strike, slushed through snow, gorged on giant pretzels, met actors... and at night? My roomie, Rose Mary, answered questions.

As a debate coach, it was my job to make sure my team prepared both sides. On one side of a legal pad you write *Affirmative,* on the other *Negative*. You draw a line down the center, and basically argue with yourself until you have exhausted every possibility. In some circles, people who argue with themselves get medication; in debate, if done correctly, you get a trophy.

I was certain I could construct the perfect question to 'catch her' or have the 'thesis' crumble, but it didn't happen. Nope. Not once. I would say, "Oh yeah? Well what about this? Or this?" And she'd answer. No crumble. No catching. It felt right. It was logical. It was truth.

A trophy.

Before the week was up, Rose Mary received a telephone call from her husband Dennis that his mother had passed away. I watched as her daughter Melenie heard the news, and although she was saddened by her grandmother's death, there was a peaceful acceptance that puzzled me. My experiences with death were very different from this. A kind of comfort filled our hotel room as Rose Mary and her daughter shared treasured stories about the woman who suffered with physical limitations on earth, but was now 'made whole'. They made plans to leave New York the following day.

At the end of the trip, as I flew back to Arizona, with the remaining students, I knew I had changed. I had tasted truth and I wanted more. Even if it cost me my marriage, I was going to find out about these Fluffies.

These Mormons.

CHAPTER 5: Driver's Test

Shortly after I arrived home, I sat Jerry down and told him that I was interested in learning about the Mormons. I asked if he wanted to do the same. He says that everything inside of him wanted to say, "No!" but when he opened his mouth, 'Yes' came out. He thinks it was the Spirit. It might have been the scotch. Either way, we were going to do this together to see where it might lead.

His words: '*You see I knew some things about what the Mormons did and some about the things they didn't do. For me the big thing was no drinking. I was a dedicated alcoholic. Although for the most part a functioning one; I didn't want to give it up. So when D said she wanted to take the lessons to learn more about being a Mormon, and asked me if I would be interested in attending them with her, I remember being scared, and what was going through my mind. Every fiber of my body and mind was going to tell her NO. But somehow the word that came out of my mouth was YES. I couldn't then and can't to this day explain why except that the Spirit was so strong and in that instant helped me understand how important this would be in our lives. I have never questioned the importance of that moment in my life.*'

After that, I called Rose Mary to tell her about our decision. Becky was with her at the time. They started to cry. I put my hand over the receiver and whispered to Jerry, “They're crying.”

Jerry gave me a questioning shrug. I've since learned Mormons cry a *lot*.

“There are lessons,” Rose Mary said.

Again, with the hand and the whispering, “There are lessons.”

Jerry rolled his eyes.

“That's fine,” I answered, figuring it was like a driver's exam. You take lessons, then a test and if you get 80%...ta dah...you're a Mormon.

“Let me make some arrangements, and I'll call you back,” Rose Mary hung up and Jerry and I stared at each other.

Our lessons were scheduled for Thursdays; first with stake missionaries, then two missionaries from ‘our’ ward. I clearly remember the first lesson. We watched an archeological film titled: *Ancient America Speaks.* As a child, I loved studying about the explorers: Desoto, Vasco de Gama, all of them.

In this film, the narrator quotes from Christopher Columbus' journals about how the ‘Indians’ were astonished that the white God, from heaven, had returned. Hmmm...*returned*? Someone had to have been somewhere in order to return to that place. Those 'tumblers' were really starting to make noise.

Each week we met with Rose Mary, Denny and the missionaries. And each week I felt more and more confident Jerry and I were doing the right thing.

One night, as we walked home discussing the lesson, Jerry stopped and said, "I know this is what you want, but I'm not so sure." He's an engineer, I told myself; he needs more 'proof.' But I was scared. Scared that I might have to back up a promise I'd made; a promise that would end our ten-year marriage – and a relationship I had counted on since I was 16.

I now understand that my husband was dealing with his own fears. It was change. Big change. Change that would take our lives in a whole new direction, and that was terrifying to him.

Then one Thursday, after getting ready for the night's lesson, we had about a half hour to kill. Jerry went into his office and decided to read from *A Marvelous Work and a Wonder, a* book that outlines the truthfulness of the restoration. In this instance, restoration refers to the Lord's church being restored as it was anciently. Randomly opening to a page, it fell to Chapter 23 – *The Sabbath Day*. Having been raised Seventh Day Adventist, Jerry had questions about this topic.

Again in Jerry's words: *'Well, it opened to the chapter about the Sabbath day and how and why it was changed to*

Sunday as a celebration of our Savior's resurrection. The Spirit right then and there was so strong and bore witness to me that this was true. I never questioned it again.'

He read what the chapter discussed, knew with a certainty of its truthfulness, closed the book, and checked his watch, noting it was exactly the time we needed to leave.

He has never looked back.

The missionaries made a date for our baptism. It was moving very fast. We hadn't even attended church. So, one Sunday, with the promise of one of Rose Mary's home-cooked meals following church, we went to our first sacrament meeting. Sacrament is similar to communion in other sects.

It was Boy Scout Sunday. Everyone was really nice...and it was Boy Scout Sunday. The building was beautifully kept, lots of great families...and did I mention it was Boy Scout Sunday?

We went again the following Sunday, Fast and Testimony Sunday...ugh! Everyone remembered our names. We shook a lot of hands. I had a new dress, and it was...Fast and Testimony Sunday! Seriously, if the gospel wasn't true, we would have never made it to week three.

You get the picture. It was just so different than anything we had experienced. What did Boy Scouts have to do with church? Why would anyone go an entire day without eating? How could we explain these to our best friends? With all this in mind, we made a conscience decision not to tell them, or my sister, who was living with us at the time. It's like announcing you're going on a diet and then never losing any weight because you can't stick with it. Everyone knows, and you end up embarrassing yourself.

Then one day our friend Geraldine approached us with, "What are you doing on Sundays? Why aren't you coming here? And why aren't you drinking? Are you becoming a Mormon?"

CHAPTER 6: What Has She Done Now?

"Yes, we are taking lessons on Thursdays and going to church on Sundays," we said. Might as well be direct. There was to be no beating around any burning bush now.

"Well, that's okay for you," was our friends' reply. "Just don't bring any of those Bible thumpers around here."

A few lessons later, as Dean and Geraldine watched the transformation of their two friends, they wanted to know how it was going 'over there.' We shared what we had recently learned about tithe. Now, I have to tell you something about my husband. When he was told the definition of tithe is 10% of a person's income, his first question was, "Is that gross or net?"

When we explained to them we were going to pay tithe, Geraldine turned to Jerry and said, "What has she done now?"

As we continued with the lessons, and with church, Geraldine and Dean eventually decided if we were going through with this Mormon thing then, as our friends, they should learn something about it and asked to come to a lesson.

These are *really* good friends.

The following Thursday Dean and Geraldine sat in with us, Rose Mary, Denny and the missionaries. We were baptized on June 12, 1980. Two months later, Dean and Geraldine were baptized as well.

Geraldine writes:

'The only reason I started investigating the church was to see what my friends, D. Ann and Jerry, were doing. They were in church on Sunday for 3 hours instead of drinking and playing cards with my husband and me.

We started the lessons with the ward missionaries. I would answer the door with a cigarette in one hand and a glass of wine in the other. After a short time I realized that I was learning about the church. They wanted to completely change my life. At first I was having none of it.

As Lanny and Tim (ward missionaries) shared the lessons and their testimonies, my feelings changed. I realized that what they were saying was true. I managed (with much difficulty) to quit drinking and smoking. I was baptized and my life changed.

Before joining the church I did not want to bring children into the world. It was too chaotic and unpredictable. Now I have a daughter and son. As I write this I can hear my 4 grandchildren splashing in the pool and laughing.

I guess you could say that the church changed my life -- for the better.'

Meanwhile, my sister, still living with us, was also curious as to what was going on with us on Thursdays. Where did we disappear to? "Are you studying to be Mormons?"

"Why yes. Yes we are."

At the time, one of Jackie's concerns was the ERA – the Equal Rights Amendment. Having had issues with her previous church, in that regard, she worried there would be similar problems for Mormon women; so we invited her to church, and she accepted. As is typical in sacrament meetings, women speak on any and all gospel topics. They teach classes, hold leadership positions, are encouraged to pursue higher education, and are active, not just in family affairs, but in community and civic issues as well. This impressed Jackie; which led her to the missionaries, which in turn, led her to be baptized a few weeks after Jerry and me.

Several days before our baptism, we had interviews with the stake president, a gentle older man, whom I had never met. I went first, and was very nervous, convinced he would let my husband join, but turn me down because I wasn't good enough to be a member.

I can't recall all the things he asked, but I do remember when he came to the question concerning the Word of Wisdom – the church's health code which includes abstinence from addictive substances, I was truthful, telling him I didn't know if I could live it forever, but I knew I could live it for one more day, and then I began to cry. He sat next to me with a box of tissues and said Heavenly Father didn't need me to be perfect, just willing.

June 12th was a great day. There was a feeling of expectation as I went through my usual routines, like waiting to open Christmas presents, or going to your birthday party. From the Book of Mormon the question:

And now, behold, I ask you...have ye spiritually been born of God? Have ye received his image in your countenances? Have ye experienced a mighty change in your hearts...

Book of Mormon - Alma 5:14

That *'mighty change of heart'* had begun, and it was about to move forward with water and fire.

Our friends, ward members, my sister as well as dozens of students, most members some not, were there. I was touched by their enthusiasm and genuine joy at the occasion. One student gave a talk on prayer. Two sang. Why would anyone, much less teenagers, care so much about this?

Now I know.

Let's recap: five new converts in two months, all in the same ward. Our Bishop loved us; offered us a scholarship of 5% tithe if we would just stay in his boundaries. Okay, that last part isn't true, but the rest is.

Want to know what an alcoholic/addict asks herself the day after she is baptized, alone in her house searching a mirror for signs of fluffiness? "*What have I done now?*"

Now you're a Mormon. So what? Well, I'll tell you so what. That summer, after we joined. I made a list:

How To Be A Proper Mormon

1. Read *that* book
2. Pray every day
3. Be nice to people you don't like
4. Memorize a hymn, so instead of cussing you can sing
5. Buy another dress
6. Learn to bake bread

Except for the bread one (and let's face it, that's what Rhodes is for) and occasionally forgetting #'s 3 and 4, I finished the list.

By the time I went back to school, at the end of the summer, I had completed the Book of Mormon. I figured I'd cross it off the list, and be done with it. *Au contraire mon ami.* I began to feel overload. I had no idea what people were talking about: Melchizedek (I still have to look it up to spell it), Relief Society, family night, visiting teachers, home teachers, Aaronic, quad, ad infinitum plus a day.

Say what?

Depression set in and after church one Sunday, I lie in bed convinced I had made a huge mistake. I would never fit in. These women who sewed their children's clothes, canned fruit and carved waxed center pieces, looked like they were molded from fondant. Their family's genealogy went back five generations when Brigham Young brought their ancestors, along with tens of thousands of refugees carrying everything they owned in handcarts, across the Rockies. My ancestors came across the Mass Turnpike in a broken down station wagon.

I knelt down and said a prayer, asking Father to tell me what to do. Was this a mistake? How could I feel so certain about being baptized, only to find myself frustrated and alone? I felt impressed to pick up the Book of Mormon, opening it 'at random' (we all know what that means) and read from Mosiah 4:27:

And see that all these things are done in wisdom and order; for it is not requisite that a man should run faster than he has strength. And again, it is expedient that he should be diligent, that thereby he might win the prize; therefore, all things must be done in order.

That's how I learned that the Book of Mormon is not to be read once then displayed on the living room table to impress other members. On that Sunday, Heavenly Father not only opened that scripture for me, He opened my eyes, and church wasn't quite as ominous.

After that, I bought a student workbook from Deseret Books, and began a two-year study of the Book of Mormon. Over the last three decades, I have read it a couple dozen times and am still amazed at how much I glean from it every time I pick it up. It is truly an inspired work. It is a historical guide that teaches us about life. It comforts, guides, trains and enlightens, and yes, on occasion, it can be used to level a table leg, but that just shows you how the Book of Mormon truly serves.

CHAPTER 7: Victoria's Secret

As word got around campus that Mrs. Nadeau was thinking about becoming one of *those,* some fascinating events took place. A group of non LDS students, believing I was damned if I joined the Mormon Church, began including my name in their lunchtime prayer circle. I was flattered that they were worried about my eternal progress, but I also found it interesting that it was only *after* I had stopped drinking alcohol, coffee, swearing, and started going to church that they became concerned.

Well-meaning students, as well as adults, presented me with all kinds of reading material containing 'facts' about the Mormons. Of course more than three decades later, I know those 'facts' to be myths.

Here is a sampling of some of those myths.

1. The reason Mormons have so many kids is they believe only the seventh son of a seventh son can get to heaven. No. Don't you think that concept is a rather limited one? It'd be kind of lonely up there.
2. Latter Day Saints practice polygamy. No. I did not join a group in order to share my husband. He can't afford it, and I wouldn't tolerate it. There are groups

that have *broken off* from the church which do practice polygamy, but they are NOT part of our faith.

3. When you go to the temple you will be required to make animal sacrifice. Seriously? The cost of carpet cleaning alone would be prohibitive. So no.
4. Part of temple ritual is for missionaries to have relations with the women. No. No. No. In many areas, missionaries aren't even allowed to attend the temple while on their missions, so as not to distract from their work. I had one student whom I adored, and still do, tell me her aunt dove out of the Salt Lake temple and into the Great Salt Lake to avoid this very thing. Aunty would have to be quite a diver because the closest point of the lake from the temple is approximately ten miles.
5. Mormons worship 'magical underwear.' No we don't. Victoria has *that* secret, not us.
6. Mormon women are second-class citizens being forced to remain barefoot and pregnant. Heck no. Having spent this much time with me, do I seem like the type of woman that would allow that to happen? Really. Just ask my husband. Utah women were given the right to vote in 1895 when the state's constitution was written. Brigham Young fought for women's rights just as he encouraged women to go

to medical school, believing their innate nature to nurture would prove them excellent doctors.

I know Mormon women who are attorneys, teachers, doctors, musicians, artists, nurses, a race car driver, professional athletes, authors, and entertainers. Just like everywhere else. So why can't *you* be a priesthood holder you ask? Who cares? I've seen the job, and I don't want it. We women have plenty of other responsibilities. I, for one, am not jealous. No one gets paid. It is *all* volunteer. The average Bishop (pastor) puts in at least twenty hours a week, besides his regular work and family responsibilities. Every job in the church is important. That has never bothered me. Trust me, I am not oppressed. If there is a priesthood holder out there treating his wife, his daughters, or *any* person unjustly the Lord has counsel for that man:

That the rights of the priesthood are inseparably connected with the powers of heaven, and that the powers of heaven cannot be controlled nor handled only upon the principles of righteousness.

That they may be conferred upon us, it is true; but when we undertake to cover our sins, or to gratify our pride, our vain ambition, or to exercise control or dominion or compulsion upon the souls of the children of men, in any degree of unrighteousness, behold, the heavens withdraw themselves; the Spirit of the Lord is grieved; and when it is withdrawn, Amen to the priesthood or the authority of that man.

Doctrine and Covenants 121:36-37

There is a popular Mormon joke about a little boy who comes home from a church activity and exclaims: "I got a part in the church play. I am the Dad."

"Don't worry dear," the Mom says. "Next time you'll get a speaking part."

7. Every member of the church gets a monthly allotment from Salt Lake City. No. But if that were true, someone owes me big time. We have a very effective welfare system where those *in need* can get temporary assistance. Many members contribute to this program by volunteering in church warehouses throughout the world canning, packaging food, clothing or household needs to be distributed to

individuals in crisis or to areas where disaster has struck.

I witnessed the church's welfare/humanity programs first-hand during the tragic Laguna, California fires when over 350 homes were leveled as flames swept Laguna Canyon. Everything from medical assistance to toiletries and furnishings were provided by the church who consistently work hand in hand with other charitable organizations to help people internationally as well as locally wherever there is a need, whether they are members of the Church or not.

The funding for these programs come from fast offerings. Once a month, members who are able, fast for two consecutive meals and donate whatever the cost of those meals for charity. Many donate more than the cost.

8. Mormons are homophobes. Another no. This was not as big a concern in 1980, but it is now, and I thought this might be a good time to address it. I don't know one Mormon who would wish harm to another person whatever his or her sexual preference. I can't speak for 15,000,000 plus members of the church; I can

only speak for this one. It is true our faith is such that we do not support same-sex marriage. When the question of it arose, as a person with gay friends, I found myself in a tough spot. On the one hand I believe it isn't really any of my business what another person's preference is. We should judge a tree by the fruit it bears. On the other hand, I wanted to do what Father has told me is right.

Once again, I found myself in prayer. This time I was reminded of a sponsor I had for many years. An old-timer that had pretty much seen it all. I remember calling her, paralyzed with fear, about a loved-one making dangerous choices.

"What should I do?" I pleaded.
'Have you made your bed?"
"What?
"Have you made your bed?"
"No."
"Go make your bed then call me back."
Man was I ticked. But I was in too much pain not to do it. Afterwards I called her back.
"Have you got dishes to do?"
"What?"

"You heard me."

Back I go to do the dishes all the while making some colorful remarks about this woman's methods of sponsorship.

This went on for a few hours, until the worry had subsided and I found myself just keeping busy doing what I needed to do for me.

What I came to realize about this wise woman was that she had been where I was. She could see the end from the beginning. That's what Father was trying to tell me. I don't know what the end is, but I do know that gender assignment is important to the eternal plan. I also know with absolute certainty that Heavenly Father has never misled me.

The church has thirteen Articles of Faith, one of which states:

We believe ... in obeying, honoring, and sustaining the law.

> That doesn't mean we can't use proper channels to challenge it if we believe it to be wrong. That said, if a gay friend asked me to attend his or her wedding I would. I am grateful that we can focus on the interests we share and not the differences.

That is just a few of the 'facts' shared with me during my investigation. The list of misconceptions is extensive. It is no different from other religions. Our knowledge is only as good as our information. One of my best friends is a practicing Islam. And guess what? She is *not* a terrorist.

CHAPTER 8: Long Haul Light

One day during those early weeks as members of the church, a friend of ours from our college days in Boston came through town. He was a long haul truck driver on his way to pick up a load in California. As it happened, we were to be at Dean and Geraldine's home that evening to sit in on their second lesson, and we invited Benjamin to join us.

He recently wrote me to tell me of his experience during that visit describing how he learned how to pray. Although he had prayed his entire life, it was only after that lesson that he understood prayer's true power.

Once his brief visit was over, Benjamin left for California to pick up an especially heavy load for which he needed a special permit. The weight forced him to drive slower than usual, and at one point, he was cut off by a convertible filled with teenagers. He said a quick prayer and was blessed to avoid an accident.

Several hundred miles later, he heard on the radio that a tornado was predicted at the time and place in Texas where he was to deliver his load. Stopping for gas, he wondered if he should take the chance and continue on. While fueling his rig, he decided to say another prayer. This one would be less frantic than the first. This danger less eminent than that of the convertible.

The answer was clear; '*Spend the night. Do not go on.*' New to promptings such as this he asked again – the same response. A third try brought the same answer. Still questioning, he replaced the pump and heard the sound of water coming from underneath his truck. The water pump had burst. Now, he was being *forced* to spend the night. Benjamin writes:

The following day '*about sixty miles east of Tucson the traffic started to slow down, I shut off my radio and turned on my CB-radio, I learned that I was approaching a big wreck. The night before between 11:00 pm and midnight seven trucks in the east bound lane were in this wreck, seven drivers were killed. I started thinking, if I got my fuel, a quick meal and headed out, look at your watch, there would have been eight trucks and eight drivers in that wreck.*'

Now, do I think that somehow those truckers died because they did not pray? Of course not. I can't say why that accident happened. But I can say that I believe it was Benjamin's time to gain a testimony of prayer and Heavenly Father's plan for him and his family.

Prayer is powerful. I know He hears *all* prayers no matter how they are delivered, but when I learned the pattern used by Latter-Day Saints, it was as if my prayers had gone into overdrive. I could *feel* Him listening. I wrote the little format down on a piece of paper and kept it on my nightstand:

1. Address Heavenly Father like: Dear Heavenly Father or something similar using His name
2. Give thanks for my blessings – be specific
3. Ask for counsel – a question or comfort for a problem in my life
4. Close in the name of Jesus Christ. Amen.

I stopped using rote prayers and learned to pour my heart out. Tell Him my feelings, fears, angers, desires. It was nothing short of a miracle. So my prayer would be something like this:

Dear Heavenly Father,

Thank Thee for today's blessings. My healthy family, my home, my friends. Thank Thee for Thy love and comfort even when I don't love myself I know Thou loves me.

Please give me the courage to make the right choices when I am tempted to be unkind or selfish. Help me to see others, especially those whom I may perceive as my enemies, through Thine eyes.

I ask this in Jesus' name. Amen.

The example I gave is…well let's face it…made to make me look magnanimous. Hey, I'm the one writing the story. It is, by my own admission, an idealized version of most of my invocations, but I have learned that it's okay to pray about big decisions as well as little ones. If it is important to me, it is important to Him. I have sought His counsel for a wayward family member, which house to buy, how to repair a friendship, a sick child, an angry co-worker. He is my Father. He is perfect and kind and His love is unconditional. He may say 'no,' He may say 'yes.' He may not answer immediately because it is not the time, or I need to seek more information. I need to do my homework, then lay out my plan in order for Him to confirm it or reject it. I understood the adage, 'God helps those who help themselves.' In addition, I now know that:

Faith without works is dead...

James 2:26.

It made sense. If Heavenly Father is the perfect parent then He wants me to grow and to become my best me. How many times has your child come to you for money to purchase something he or she *has to have* that they will remain interested in for all of twenty seconds? You say 'yes,' then hand him a rake. It's good parenting. Yes, yes I know, sometimes we just give him the money to get it over with because we know we will probably have to re-rake the yard anyway, or apologize to the neighbors for having our leaves blown into their pool. Oh yeah, it happens! But you and I know the rake route is the better lesson. Father knows that as well. He knows what we are capable of and wants us to:

Be ye therefore perfect, even as your Father which is in heaven is perfect.

Matt. 5:48.

No one, not even politicians or actors, no matter how much money they spend on campaigns or publicity, will reach perfection in this life. What is important is the process during our time on earth. To be continually moving forward, even when we take two steps backwards and simply hand the kid 20 bucks.

'But truly our Father knows us and hears the pleadings of our hearts. He accomplishes His miracles one prayer at a time, one person at a time. We can trust that He will help us, not necessarily in the way we want but in the way that will best help us to grow. Submitting our will to His may be difficult, but it is essential to becoming like Him and finding the peace He offers us.'

—Jean A. Stevens, *Fear Not; I Am with Thee*

A humble trucker took the time to sit in on a lesson. He felt something, and decided to put what he heard to the test. Benjamin talks about his life today with his five beautiful children and his twelve grandchildren, all active members of the church, many of whom serve in leadership positions.

Like I said, prayer is powerful.

CHAPTER 9: I Have Your Name on Me

Jerry and I could not have children. We tried…a lot. I miscarried several times, and was finally told it was not possible for us to carry full term. That was before In Vitro. Maybe now it would be different. Of course, at my age, 'maybe now' would be a miracle.

One Friday night, six months after joining the church, we received a phone call from our friend Denny, an attorney. That day, a young woman had come into his office to see one of Denny's partners who, it turns out, was not in. She tried the second partner – same thing. Finally, she met Denny and said she wanted to designate an LDS couple for her unborn baby and asked if he could help her. That night he gave us a call.

"Think about it over the weekend, and call me Sunday night," he said.

We promised, and hung up. Jerry was certain, and suggested we say yes right away. That was unusual for him because he really hadn't wanted children. I was the one who longed for us to be parents, but now it was I who wasn't so sure. We were sober, not fighting; we had good friends, and a better life. I didn't want anything to tip the scales. Before bed that night we knelt down together and asked Father what to do. While I slept, I had a dream and in it a baby came to me – I couldn't tell if it was a boy or a girl – but this tiny, beautiful person smiled at me and said these words: *'I have your name on me, and I have been waiting a long time, and I'm coming.'*

I woke Jerry early the next morning, "We have to tell Denny yes," I said.

"Really? It's a big decision and we have another day,"

"No, it's right. We have to call," and so we did.

"Are you sure?" Denny asked. We told him we were, hung up, and waited two long months. During that time our tender testimonies were put to the test. We prayed fervently every night and several times throughout each day.

Our son was born on a Wednesday February 4, 1981. The law stated we had to wait 72 hours before we could pick him up from the hospital. The Friday before the appointed day I took a call in my office from Jerry who had just gotten off the phone with Denny. The birth mother had asked to see the baby. In most cases that does not bode well for the adoptive parents. I was devastated, and after hanging up, closed my office door to pray (it seems I pray a lot). While I prayed, a peaceful feeling filled the room; I felt the presence of Jackie's late father (she is my half-sister), and was impressed that all would be well. It was.

The next day we drove to the hospital and waited nervously in the lobby while Denny and Rose Mary went up to get our son and deliver him to us. For me after that, 'time stood still' was more than a trite saying. When I finally saw him, and held him in my arms, it felt comfortable like we had known each other forever.

Honestly? There have been some days when I said, "What was I thinking? This is too hard and I demand a recount." But I know that he is ours, and all that we have learned as parents – the mistakes, the joys, and the pain – have helped to make us who we are. All of it is designed to bring us back to Father as a family.

One year to the day that we were baptized, Jerry and I went to the Mesa temple to be sealed. A temple sealing is an ordinance performed by proper priesthood authority that unites a man and woman together for time and all eternity, not just '*til death do us part*.' Those not given the chance, here on earth to be sealed, can have it done for them by members of the church who attend the temple for such purposes. I have felt the presence of many of my deceased relatives as Jerry and I stood in for them. What an amazing feeling to be able to bring loved ones together in this way.

At our own sealing, kneeling across from each other, we were surrounded by many of the same people who loved and supported us through our conversion. That little space, off the Celestial room, felt like Heavenly Father was holding Jerry and I under His arm as we made the simple covenants that bound us for time and all eternity. After we were sealed to each other, a temple attendant brought our baby, sound asleep and dressed in a mini white jumpsuit, into us. We each placed our hand on him, as beautiful words were spoken to make him ours, now not just legally, but forever. That spirit, who came to me through the haze of my dream, would truly bear our name. For better or worse, we are an eternal unit.

CHAPTER 10: Are You Looking for Something to Read?

Shortly after we were sealed, we decided to fly back to Boston and introduce our son to the family, and while we were there we would introduce them to the gospel, making sure everybody was baptized before we left. Hey, it had worked for the five of us, why not them?

Well, I packed up our suitcases, and along with everything else I included copies of the Book of Mormon, Joseph Smith tracts in both English and Spanish (at the time I didn't even know anyone who spoke Spanish, but I was prepared). I also included anything else that could be useful in our missionary efforts, making sure I put a few of those items in our carry-on, now upgraded to a diaper bag.

Our flight was a red-eye (no first class this time) starting in Phoenix with one stop in Atlanta, Georgia. It was one of those big planes, like a 747 where there are five seats in the center, and two on either side. I was in the middle seat of the middle section; Jerry was to my right, and our son shared laps somewhere between us.

To my left, was a Marine coming back from R&R – a lot of R&R. He was *very* tired. To his left, on the aisle seat, was a man who looked like he might be from India. The flight went on, our baby cried, the Marine snored, the Indian read. It got late.

Finally, all the lights were out, and the passengers had settled in to sleep. I tried, but kept getting this feeling that I was to share something with someone, but who? I prayed. The Indian went to the bathroom. Okay, not him. I tapped the Marine on his shoulder. He grunted and went back to sleep. Okay, not him either. I prayed again, and the feeling was still there. Still strong. The Indian came back, turned his overhead light on, and started looking through his seat pocket for something to read. I leaned forward, "Are you looking for something to read?"

"Why yes, I am," he said, his voice dignified and soft.

I whipped out the Joseph Smith Testimony tract and handed it to him, "Here, read this." Then leaning back in my seat I hyperventilated while watching him from the corner of my eye. He was one of those people who reads quickly, like scanning a shopping list. When he was finished I heard myself ask, "What do you think?"

"Is this true?"

"It is," I said.

He looked at me and spoke the following five words, "I want to be baptized."

Every time I tell this story to a group of missionaries I can almost hear them sigh collectively while shaking their fists at me, "Give me a break lady."

I want to be baptized? Okay, now I am wide awake and practically laying across the Marine's lap. "Well, there's a book.

I can send it to you." By this time, the plane is beginning its descent and the passengers have to prepare for landing. We have only enough time to exchange names and addresses before disembarking.

His name is Carl, and he is from Trinidad, part of the West Indies, a series of islands off the coast of Venezuela. I tell him we will be back in Arizona in two weeks, and I will make sure he gets the book. The four of us part. Jerry and I grin at each other like we swallowed the proverbial canary. Actually, we had just eaten airline food, so maybe we did.

We visited our families, showed off the kid, swam, barbequed, laughed, reminisced, even went to church. What we didn't do was go to any baptisms. That's okay. Even though both families were at first cautious, they have come to understand our faith is part of who we are. They are good, generous people, who were and are an important part of our lives.

In the midst of our visit we would think of Carl, somewhere out there on his island hopefully re-reading his pamphlet in anticipation of the Book of Mormon coming in the mail. When we arrived home there was a letter waiting for us from Trinidad.

Carl wrote: *'God surely does work in a miraculous way! A plane departed from San Diego to Phoenix, thence to Atlanta. There was one solitary person aboard who was searching for a meaning to life. Then, there came a family who happened to be seated close to him. He never knew them nor they him but God did it! She, the lady, handed that lonely man a booklet about the testimony of the prophet Joseph Smith. That was it! He had found a meaning to life! What a miracle.'*

Continuing to write throughout the rest of the summer and into the fall, Carl told us he'd saved for a long time to come to the States. He had been searching for the truth, and believed if there was one place to find it, it would be in the United States. His sister lived in San Diego, and he had spent his time there hoping something or someone would show him what he was looking for. He was leaving heart-broken, and just before I handed him that pamphlet, Carl had gone into the bathroom to kneel down in prayer asking God why He had not answered his questions. So, when Carl read about Joseph Smith, he knew he had found the truth. His prayers were heard.

CHAPTER 11: Lee Iacocca

This was exciting news. We couldn't wait to call our missionaries and tell them what was happening. I sent off the Book of Mormon, and filled out one of those referral slips for church headquarters in Salt Lake City. We didn't hear from them, but we did hear from Carl – a lot.

'I hear there is a song book. Can I have one?'

'I heard about *A Marvelous Work and a Wonder* by Le Grand Richards. Would you send me one of those?'

Of course we did. I remember going to people in the stake asking if they could donate some books to send to Trinidad. We packaged up a bunch of stuff, filled out another referral slip and waited. Nothing from Salt Lake City – lots from Carl.

Finally, I wrote Carl wanting to know what was going on down there with all those books. He wrote back to tell us that on Sundays, he and thirteen of his friends met in his apartment to sing hymns, read from the books we sent them, and have discussions about what they read. They called it, *The Church of Jesus Christ Of Latter-Day Saints Sunday School*, and wanted to know when the missionaries were coming. Soon, I assured him.

Frustrated, having not heard from Salt Lake City, I decided that if I had a problem with my Chrysler, and couldn't get any satisfaction, I would write to Lee Iacocca, the president and CEO of the company at the time. So, in this case, I wrote to the President of *our* company – Spencer W. Kimball. I didn't know you weren't supposed to do that.

President Kimball wrote back:

THE CHURCH OF JESUS CHRIST OF LATTER-DAY SAINTS
47 EAST SOUTH TEMPLE STREET
SALT LAKE CITY, UTAH 84150

SPENCER W. KIMBALL, PRESIDENT

September 2, 1981

Mrs. Dorothy Nadeau

Dear Sister Nadeau:

I thank you very kindly for your letter and for your sweet testimony which you have shared with me. Thanks, also, for the letter and testimony of Brother Carl which you enclosed. How wonderful!

Your expressions of love and support are very much appreciated, as are your prayers in my behalf. I am pleased and delighted with the news of your letter and the many blessings you have received since you accepted the gospel. I was especially interested in the conversion story of strangers who met on an airplane, of a man who read the testimony of the Prophet Joseph Smith, and who believed at once!

Please be assured of my love and blessings, which I extend to you and your husband, and to your new little boy, with my kindest wishes.

Faithfully yours,

Spencer W. Kimball
President

Nowhere did the prophet state that missionaries would be immediately dispatched to Trinidad, West Indies per my request.

Hmmph! The nerve.

I continued to assure Carl, and I continued to fill out those referral slips. One day, as God would have it, I met someone who said she knew the Branch President (a branch is smaller than a ward) in Trinidad. She gave me his number and I called. The Branch President said it was difficult for missionaries, at that time, because the government was run mostly by men of African descent, who were, understandably, suspicious of the church. This was 1981; the declaration to allow blacks to hold the Priesthood had only come in 1978. He also said that Carl's apartment was only about a mile from where they met for church, and he would visit him as soon as possible.

Early the following year, in a beautiful setting, Carl and other faithful Trinidadians were baptized as members of The Church of Jesus Christ of Latter-Day Saints.

What a remarkable show of faith, for one man to be so determined to *'bring the world His truth'* (hymn 172, *Children's Songbook*). Carl and I lost contact for many years until we recently found each other on...of course...Facebook. He still has that pamphlet, still shares the gospel with others, and is still an incredible man.

Note: *All you missionaries out there banging on doors? Just hop a coast to coast flight, and you'll have a captive audience.*

CHAPTER 12: I'll Do What You Want Me to Do

You want to know something else about being a new convert? Well, even if you don't, you've come this far with me, so why not ask?

Okay, what is something else about being a new convert?

Aw, thanks for asking.

Not only do you want to change who you are, you want to change who you *were*. Or, at least I did. I never wanted to tell anyone about my past. I wanted to come from that family I saw in Sacrament meetings. Those Fluffies who said nice things to each other, never drank caffeinated drinks, and thought flavored gelatin was a garden salad.

I bought clothes with puffy sleeves, framed every picture and print resembling pioneers slogging through mud or snow. I signed up for multi-level sales, and made sure every doctor, insurance agent and plumber I dealt with had a current temple recommend.

It was exhausting.

One day, during this phase of white-knuckling perfectionism, a seminary teacher approached me to ask if I would spend a day talking to each class about my conversion. Many LDS high school students take a four year Seminary course to study what we refer to as the Standard Works – Old Testament, New Testament, Book of Mormon and Doctrine and Covenants (Doctrine and Covenants is church history and modern day revelations). Sometimes it is before school, but in areas where there are large numbers of LDS students, it can be done at a release-time during the school day.

I told the local seminary teacher I would love to talk to his students and got permission to take a personal day from work. I then spent the week before preparing what I was going to say. Fun, practical stories, with a human touch; with any luck the kids would feel the Spirit, cry and I'd be a huge success. It was a brilliant plan. I was excited, right up until the first group of students walked in.

I watched in horror as one of my students, who I had no idea was a member, entered. He was a sophomore, and in trouble most of the time. Having had similar experiences, I could tell by his behaviors what was going on with him. This boy was doing some of the things I wanted to forget; and trying to be a good example, I did not want him to believe:

...there is no harm in this...God will beat us with a few stripes, and at last we shall be saved in the kingdom of God.

Book of Mormon - 2 Nephi 28:8

Now what?

During the opening exercises, I went into the ladies' room to ask Heavenly Father what to do. Okay, He wasn't *literally* in the ladies' room; it was like Carl on the plane. While there, I said a quick prayer asking Father how I was to handle this, but didn't feel impressed as to what to do. I went back to the group now assembled, preparing for opening exercises. I sat down, but I was nervous, just wanting to flee, to make some excuse and go home. Finally, the class began to sing, and within seconds my answer came in the form of a hymn:

I'll go where you want me to go, dear Lord'
Over mountain or plain or sea;
I'll say what you want me to say, dear Lord;
I'll be what you want me to be.

Hymn 270, LDS Hymnal

This talk might have been *my* story, but it wasn't about me, it was about those kids understanding the importance of their example, of living the gospel no matter who was watching or what anyone thought of them. It was their example that brought me to the church as well as my husband, our friends, my sister, our son, those brave members in the West Indies and whoever else had been influenced.

I talked about my past. I didn't need to sensationalize or go into detail. I just needed to say: This is who I was. This is who I am trying to become. I made sure they understood that I didn't have the gospel in my life as a child. They could use me to rationalize their present behaviors, but it wouldn't work. Because:

> *For of him unto whom much is given much is required…*
>
> Doctrine and Covenants 82:3

And that boy? He ended up going on a mission. Was it because of me? Absolutely not. Heavenly Father knew His child's needs, knew that His child was making decisions about his life that could affect his salvation. Heavenly Father made sure it was *that* song at *that* time, and I was lucky enough to be the one there to deliver His message, not *my* message, but *His* message; just as I'm sure that boy, now a man, delivered the same message to those whom he served.

What I have learned about my past is this: although I have made mistakes, I am not a mistake. My past is best used to guide my future, to help others along the way. I am not proud of the things I have done, but I am grateful that the Lord has promised to:

> *… make weak things become strong …*
>
> Book of Mormon - Ether 12:27

CHAPTER 13: The Bridal Gown

I was directing a play called Brigadoon. Part of the story takes place in a magical land in Ireland during the 1700's. In one scene, there is a wedding where a bridal gown is needed that must be appropriate for that period.

One day a cast member came to rehearsal carrying a large box. "My Dad was clearing out an apartment he manages and the tenant left this behind," he said. "She didn't want it. If it doesn't work, just put it in the costume closet."

I opened the box to find a modern bridal gown, not really what was needed for the play; however, a strong feeling came over me that my sister Jackie was going to wear that very gown for her own wedding. It didn't make any sense, because one Sunday, a year before, Jackie had come home from a visit with her Bishop, and announced she was going on a mission. What? She had just passed her Pharmacy exam, had a decent job, and was making good friends in the ward. What was she thinking? What was her Bishop thinking? Why hadn't anyone consulted me? I closed the box, and when I went home that day, stuck it under my bed and forgot about it.

Shorty after all the papers were submitted, Jackie got her call to McAllen, Texas Spanish speaking mission. After her eighteen months in Texas, she wanted to visit our mother, and our mother's current husband, John (this one stuck – they were married for over 40 years when my mother passed away). During that time, the three of them decided to take a trip across the country stopping in a Chicago suburb to visit some of John's ex in-laws from his deceased first wife.

The last time these families had seen each other was fifteen years before when the Chicago clan went to Boston. During that visit, their fifteen year-old son Bill and my then fourteen-year old sister Jackie had a little summertime crush. When the vacation ended, they wrote for a while, but distance and age divided them, and they lost touch.

Fast forward fifteen years when the families reunited. At hearing that Jackie had just completed a mission for The Church of Jesus Christ of Latter-Day Saints, Bill's mother was astonished.

"That's the church our son, Bill, joined."

Two years before, Bill heard the gospel, and was baptized, but had become inactive after pressure from friends kept him from sharing what he knew to be true. When he saw Jackie, after all that time, and how strong she was in her beliefs, he knew he wanted the gospel back in his own life.

After an extended vacation with our parents, Jackie returned to Mesa, while she and Bill continued a long-distance telephone courtship before unlimited calling was invented. Seriously, it was just cheaper for them to get married.

So they did.

As the wedding plans began, I remembered the bridal gown, pulled it out from under the bed to have Jackie try it on. She looked beautiful, and aside from one minor repair, it didn't need a thing. It fit her as if it was made for her, which it was. That bridal gown was Father's wedding present to one of His faithful daughters who listened to a call from Him and served a mission.

On February 11, 1984, Jackie and Bill were sealed in the Mesa, Arizona temple. It was the same temple where a few years prior, I had been sealed to my husband and son.

How aware He is of everything in our lives.

...all things are created and made to bear record of me ...

Pearl of Great Price - Moses 6:63

Even a bridal gown.

CHAPTER 14: Drinking Poison

'*To err is human…to forgive*' – next to impossible. At least that has been my experience. Growing up with rage, never feeling safe or important, took root in my psyche. I still have days when the old resentments take a bite out of my peace of mind. But there is one huge resentment that Father blessed me to let go.

One of my stepfather's was a tyrant. He did not spare the rod. He needed things to be a certain way, and heaven help me if they were not. I remember being a nervous wreck whenever he would stand over me to make sure whatever task I was doing was exactly the way he thought it should be done. He died when I was in junior high, and I have to say I was happy. But life didn't get better for me. If anything, it got worse. When a child grows up without consistency or security she may find it in other places, and in other ways.

After experiencing some rough times, I came to the church and my life got so much better. But my bitterness did not readily dissipate. At times it affected other relationships. I joined a 12-step support group and began a decades-long study that led me to a greater understanding of how the Lord could help me live a better life.

One of my assignments required I write out my life's story to date, making sure to be honest in my assessment of those things I had done to add to my problems. When I got to the part of my history involving this man, I knew I needed to forgive him in order to move on. I wrote and wrote; finally, at one point I could literally feel a weight fly from my shoulders. I was free, and I was feeling pretty good about myself. How great was I that I could forgive this man who had been so abusive to me! Jerry even did my stepfather's temple work. Boy, was I righteous! What a great example. Just ask me.

Then one day (it always starts with one day, doesn't it?), I was making my bed, and got an overwhelming sense I was to kneel down and ask Father what He wanted from me. The last time I had that feeling, and I prayed about it, I was called to teach early morning Seminary. In Colorado. At 5:45 in the morning. In the snow. In the ice. Uphill. Both ways. Needless to say, it took me three days to ask Him what He wanted this time.

As soon as I knelt and asked the question, I felt words boring into my heart, "Ask your stepfather to forgive *you*."

This had to be a joke. The dark side was chiding me. But I knew. I had felt the gentle promptings of His voice before, of the Holy Ghost communicating with me. I thought about what was being asked. It was true. I owed him an apology. He had done some pretty mean things, but so had I. I had told anyone who would listen about how abusive he was, oftentimes exaggerating. So, I knelt down once again, and this time I prayed that Heavenly Father, through my Savior, would forgive me for the wrongs I had done this man. I felt complete relief. There was nothing left for which to be angry. I had picked up one end of the forgiveness stick without realizing the other end would come up with it. Now, it was complete and I am grateful to have learned such a powerful lesson.

It is said that holding on to resentment is like drinking poison thinking the other person will die. There are more events and people that seriously affected me, some, a lot worse than what my stepfather's actions did. Only if the results of such experiences cause me and the people around me to be unhappy do I work with Father to let them go.

If I dwelt on it, I could come up with a whole list of reasons to be resentful. I choose not to do that. Most situations aren't worth it. Also, the neat thing about getting older is you forget why you were angry in the first place.

But as oft as they were repented and sought forgiveness, with real intent, they were forgiven.

Book of Mormon - Moroni 6:8.

CHAPTER 15: The Dang It Effect

You know, brethren, that a very large ship is benefited very much by a very small helm in the time of a storm, by being kept workways with the wind and the waves.

Doctrine and Covenants 123:16

I was the ship in the storm, and looking back on it, there were two seemingly very small helms that helped me keep on course to find my way to shore. Both involved students.

The first was an LDS boy named John who worked on Stage Crew. He and another crew member came first thing in the morning to work on whatever sets needed building or whatever shows were being set up. If nothing was going on I would oftentimes take the boys to breakfast. One such morning, during the time I was investigating the church, we were sitting in a restaurant and John sat across from me reading the newspaper. The waitress came over; myself and the second student ordered coffee. As she walked away, I called after her, "Uhm, make that orange juice instead," I said. John tipped the corner of his newspaper down and winked at me. To this day, when I remember that second in time, I am touched at his genuine concern. He was aware of what I was trying to do, and cared about my choices.

The second incident involved a heavy door next to my office. This door led into the classroom and was one of those doors, if you didn't hold it, it slammed behind you knocking anything out of your hands like books, lunch or a soda. At least once a week, I'd hear the shouts and language of a major tragedy taking place at that door.

I have to admit, when I first started investigating the church, I was looking for the 'chink in the armor.' These kids must live secret 'other' lives especially this one LDS girl, who, to be honest, was a pain. I was convinced she was meeting 'bad boys' on the sly and watching R-rated movies when her parents weren't home. (And for all of you kids out there actually doing that – cut it out.)

One day, this particular girl was not aware that I was behind her as we walked across campus to the theatre. She was loaded with books, and I was certain, as soon as that door hit her from behind, those books would tumble down, her true colors would show, and she would start swearing. Sure enough, the door slammed, the books sprawled everywhere and I waited for the mask to come off revealing her real self. But this girl, this nuclear thorn in my side said, "Dang it!" That's it. Simply, "Dang it."

At that instant, something happened to me; a major paradigm shift took place, and I knew all of it was true: the First Vision, the Book of Mormon, all of it.

Years later, Jerry's job took us to Colorado, where, as I said previously, I was called to teach early morning Seminary. One day, I was trying to create a lesson about how our actions can affect those who watch us. So, I made a kind of genealogy chart starting with Jerry and I, adding our friends, Jackie and her husband, Benjamin and his wife, and all of our children. I added in the baptisms Jackie had on her mission, as well as those influenced by Carl's testimony in Trinidad. I pretended that all of the adults had temple recommends, and went to the temple six times a year. I knew these figures were idealistic so after all that, I cut the total in half. The result was over 5,000 people affected because two teenagers lived their values.

One of them may have been a pain, but she was a pain who stood for what she believed. By the way, that young girl was one of the two students who sang at our baptism.

I revised the chart a short time ago, using the same very unscientific formula and this time came up with over 10,000 people. Even if I cut *that* number in half a *second* time, it still left a 25% success rate, and again over 5,000 people.

That rudder, a little nothing in the middle of an enormous ocean, is exactly what will guide us home if we steer it '*workaways*' throughout our lives.

Remembering those early days when everything was so new and I was scared and excited, all at the same time, has helped confirm that the choice I made all those years ago was right.

Jesus is the Christ. He did what is said of Him. If He didn't, nothing matters. If He did, everything matters. He did. I know it as sure as there are words on this page. He is the Messiah. The One promised, and He will return. This is His church. Ancient Christianity has been restored with all its truth and covenants. The Savior spoke to His disciples:

And other sheep I have, which are not of this fold: them also I must bring, and they shall hear my voice; and there shall be one fold, and one shepherd.

John 10:16

After His sacrifice, that promise was fulfilled. He appeared in the Americas to make certain:

Joseph is a fruitful bough, even a fruitful bough by a well; whose branches run over the wall:

Genesis 49:22.

We are those branches whose ancestors have crossed oceans (walls) to be restored.

Another Joseph, Joseph Smith, was chosen to be a prophet and martyred for his belief; he was foreordained to help

Heavenly Father restore the gospel in this last dispensation of time.

There is a modern-day prophet on the earth today just as there was then. He is at the head of the Lord's true church, and receives revelation from Him to guide us in these last days. And why wouldn't there be? If there really is a God, why would He leave us to flounder by ourselves without guidance or leadership?

God gave us the Bible, and now The Book of Mormon. They do not contradict. They dovetail to bring the world all the truth there is at this time.

This is my story and my testimony. There are so many more chapters I could write. So many more miracles, but this is the gist of it. As I re-read my story, it becomes clear to me that at every juncture of this journey, whenever I needed an answer, I prayed. The same is true of the faithful friends and family who joined us along the way. They too prayed.

My sweet friend Dean recently wrote: '*I had fasted for 2 days...I was reading the bible and prayed. That's it.*'

He's right. In order to know the truth, one only has to ask with sincerity. At the end of the Book of Mormon is a challenge an ancient prophet writes:

And when ye shall receive these things, I would exhort you that ye would ask God, the Eternal Father, in the name of

Christ, if these things are not true; and if ye shall ask with a sincere heart, with real intent, having faith in Christ, he will manifest the truth of it unto you, by the power of the Holy Ghost.

And by the power of the Holy Ghost ye may know the truth of all things.

Book of Mormon - Moroni 10:4-5

My words may not be eloquent, but I stand by what I say here. A quote from the title page of the Book of Mormon may help explain how I feel:

And now, if there are faults they are the mistakes of men; wherefore, condemn not the things of God…

Thank you for taking the time to read my little book. I am grateful for you. I have been in rooms where it is said to: 'Take what you like and leave the rest.' I say, 'Take what you like and *file* the rest.' It just may come in handy some day.

These things I bear witness to you in my Savior's name, even Jesus Christ. Amen.

For further information or questions regarding The Church of Jesus Christ of Latter Day Saints you may want to visit:

- Mormon.org
- Mormonsandgays.org

Thank you for reading our little book. We hope you enjoyed it and would love for you to write a review.

WRITE YOUR REVIEW

1. Go to: http://bit.ly/SoManyMiraclesreview
2. You may post your review using your real name or choose another name.

LIKE US ON FACEBOOK

https://www.facebook.com/SoManyMiracles

D. Ann Nadeau, Author
So Many Miracles

Made in the USA
San Bernardino, CA
21 January 2020